Illuminated Designs

WITHDRAWN FROM
ST HELENS COLLEGE LIBRARY

ST.
BRO
07

22.

Don

D0491507

69849

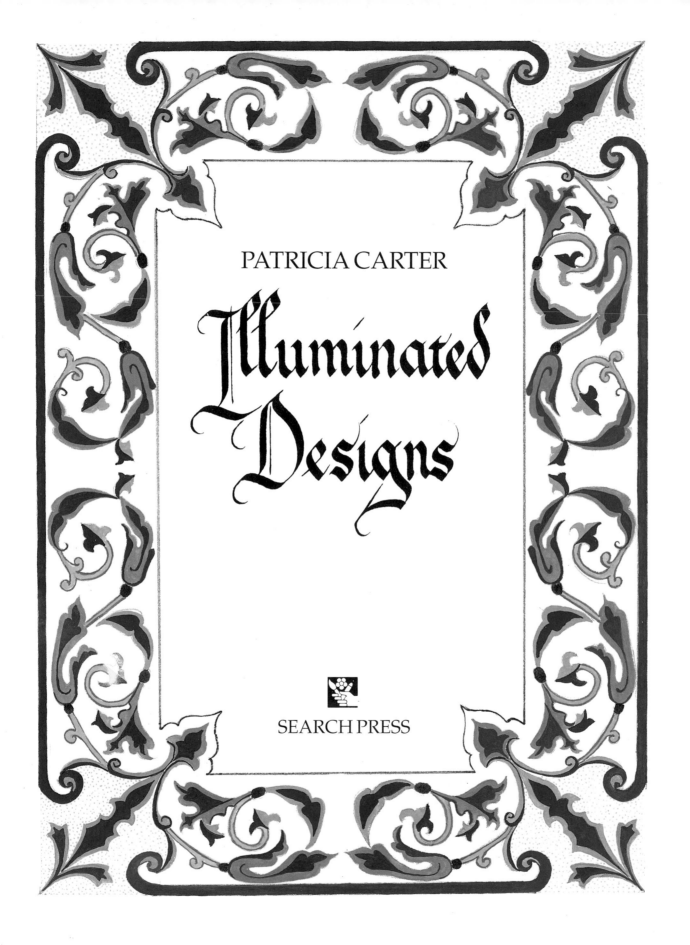

PATRICIA CARTER

Illuminated Designs

SEARCH PRESS

First published in Great Britain 1994

Search Press Limited
Wellwood, North Farm Road,
Tunbridge Wells, Kent TN2 3DR

Copyright © Patricia Carter 1994

Verses and incidental Calligraphy by Anne Gardner
Copyright © Search Press Ltd. 1994

All rights reserved. No part of this book, text, photographs or illustrations,
may be reproduced or transmitted in any form or by any means by print,
photoprint, microfilm, microfiche, photocopier, or in any way known or
as yet unknown, or stored in a retrieval system, without written
permission obtained beforehand from Search Press.

ISBN 0 85532 777 4

ST. HELENS
COLLEGE

745.61

√3960

- DEC 1994

LIBRARY

Colour Separation by P&W Graphics, Singapore
Printed in Spain by Elkar S. Coop, 48012 Bilbao

Contents

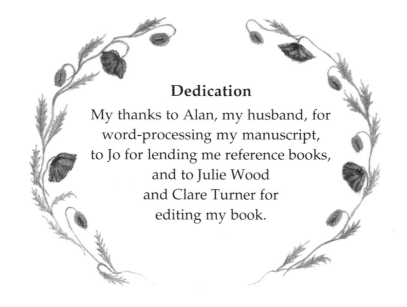

Dedication
My thanks to Alan, my husband, for
word-processing my manuscript,
to Jo for lending me reference books,
and to Julie Wood
and Clare Turner for
editing my book.

Introduction

In my previous books, *Illuminated Calligraphy* and *Illuminated Alphabets*, I tried to show you how simple it can be to create your own designs and alphabets to complement your calligraphy.

In *Illuminated Designs* I would like to show you easy ways of extending your designs to encompass such subjects as title pages, greetings cards, place cards, monograms, ciphers, writing paper, labels, invitations, paperweights, menus, bookplates, bookmarks and colophons.
This is a wide range, and so I can touch only lightly on each of these subjects, but it will give you a good idea how to begin, and I hope it will also whet your appetite to further your interest in decorative designs to accompany your calligraphy.

Inspiration may arise from the type of work that is required at the time: for instance, you may wish to give someone a wedding or christening album. Adding a personal touch and creating a personal design, including your own handwritten greeting, will enhance any gift. The designs need not be elaborate: simplicity sometimes says much more than an over-decorated page.

Most of the designs in this book are for those of you who already have a certain amount of experience in calligraphy and wish to learn something about the decorative side of the art to add interest and beauty to your work.
I hope you will find something here to suit you, to interest you enough to create your own designs. I am sure you will find this challenging art-form as fascinating and fulfilling as I do, whether as a hobby or indeed as a profession!

Materials

For the beginner learning calligraphy or designing borders for calligraphy, the amount of equipment need be minimal. A start can be made with a good set of nibs and a penholder (or a fountain pen with interchangeable nibs) and a good box of artist's-quality watercolour paints. Later on you may wish to add gouache or acrylics.

Brushes

Watercolour brushes in various sizes (Nos. 000–4) are ideal for detailed work.

Working surface

You will also require a smooth, stout board to work on: try raising it at one end with a couple of books to give yourself a good angle. Plywood will do, but if you are lucky enough to possess a small desktop drawing board, so much the better.

Paper and parchment

There is a seemingly endless range of paper available: a type to suit every medium. You can buy it in a variety of surfaces, from smooth to rough. For the purposes of this book I used acid-free 150gsm (70lb) cartridge paper. I also keep inexpensive copy paper to use when planning my designs.

Vellum and parchments are the traditional surfaces, but as they are expensive and more difficult to work on I would suggest using paper until you are more proficient.

Pencils

You will need a few different sorts. H pencils are the hardest and B the softest; there is also an F, which does not smudge as much as a B.

I use 2H and 2B pencils when tracing designs, 3B for transferring designs, and 2B when working on vellum and parchment.

I never use a coloured eraser to rub out pencil

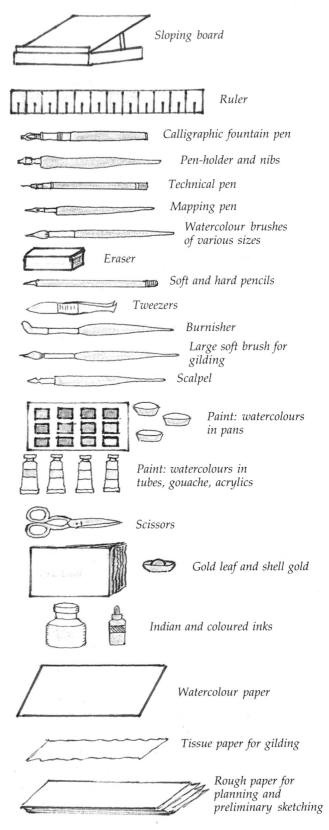

Sloping board

Ruler

Calligraphic fountain pen

Pen-holder and nibs

Technical pen

Mapping pen

Watercolour brushes of various sizes

Eraser

Soft and hard pencils

Tweezers

Burnisher

Large soft brush for gilding

Scalpel

Paint: watercolours in pans

Paint: watercolours in tubes, gouache, acrylics

Scissors

Gold leaf and shell gold

Indian and coloured inks

Watercolour paper

Tissue paper for gilding

Rough paper for planning and preliminary sketching

lines. A good white one is better, because I have found that coloured ones can stain the surface of the paper.

Inks

I use a number of inks, some waterproof and some non-waterproof, for calligraphy. Coloured inks are inclined to fade, so I would suggest not using them for any artwork you would like to be long-lasting.

Gold

For gilding you will need gold size or gum ammoniac (both are sold in liquid form in jars) as a base for your gold leaf. Gold leaf is sold in books, backed on tissue paper. Shell gold is sold in a small plastic box. You will find instructions on gilding on page 11.

Other materials

You might find the following useful: geometry equipment, a set-square, blotting paper, a pair of compasses, and stencils. You will not really *need* these to start off with: you can get them later on.

Choosing paints

Gouache

Gouache, which is opaque, is a lot easier to use for the beginner than watercolour because it does not streak like watercolour does, and it allows you to correct mistakes, which is far more difficult in watercolour.

You can buy gouache ready-made in tubes, and in a variety of colours. In fact, it is best to buy the colours rather than mixing them from one another, because with gouache, mixed colours can turn out rather muddy. For illuminated designs, muddiness must be avoided at all costs! The colours must be crystal clear and very clean, otherwise the end result will not look attractive. All fine illuminated painting should be rather dainty in colour.

Watercolour

I myself tend to use mainly watercolours for painting the designs on frontispieces and all other delicate work, but I do use gouache for painting larger capital letters and some of the surrounding design.

Watercolour pencils are also very useful. Not only are they ideal for delicate work, but they are also very easy to work with for preliminary sketches. They are excellent for shading, but a little care may be required in some areas, such as highlighting on leaves or fruit.

Do remember that watercolour dries a lighter shade, while gouache dries darker: so take care when planning your colours.

Acrylics

Acrylic colours can be watered down and used in a similar way to watercolour. The beauty of acrylic paint is that you can paint over it in the same way as you can with gouache.

Acrylics should not be laid on thickly for delicate work, but should be used fluidly, as for watercolour.

General hints

Whichever medium you choose to work with, it is wise to try out your colours on a spare piece of paper first, preferably a small piece of a similar type to the one you will be working on. You can then compare the colour.

One very important rule is: always mix more colour than you think you will need! If you run out of colour it is practically impossible to match the exact colour you had before.

Colours

The choice of colour in design is very important. When you are starting out this may seem rather daunting but with a little practice with the basic primary colours – red, blue and yellow – you will see how easy it all is. I use yellow ochre, cadmium yellow, vermilion, violet, alizarin crimson, ultramarine, viridian (or alizarin green), lamp black and Chinese white.

Gold is not regarded as a colour; it is treated as a separate element (see the section on gilding on page 11).

I use a wider range of colours in gouache because a number of these paints do not mix well. When you are starting off, a basic range of colours is all you need, plus black and white and just a few auxiliary colours. Mixing your colours is fun, and you can get some surprising results using watercolours and watercolour pencils.

Do choose clear, clean, uplifting colours; that way you cannot go too far wrong.

You should be the master of your paint – and not let the paint master you!

Gilding

Gilding is all part and parcel of illuminating, especially for formal work such as memorial books, addresses, documentation, and heraldry. It is also very useful for greetings cards and on title pages for books.

Gilding, which is an art all on its own, is not too difficult to master. There are a lot of modern tools and 'sizes' to experiment with, but for the beginner I would suggest a few basic tools to start with.

Gold paint is painted straight on to whatever you have drawn or designed. Shell gold is also painted straight on to the drawing. The difference between gold paint and shell gold is that gold paint tarnishes after a while and should not be used for anything you would like to be long-lasting. Shell gold is real gold and *is* long-lasting. It is very useful for small areas, such as dots or small letters.

Gold leaf is a good all-rounder and can be applied on both small and large areas. It looks lovely and is not as expensive as you may think.

All materials can be bought from good art suppliers in London and the larger towns, many of which have a good mail-order service throughout the world.

Materials

Fine sable brush
Water gold size or gum ammoniac
Book of gold leaf
A pair of small scissors
Tweezers
Thin paper
Sharp craft knife
Soft paintbrush
Agate burnisher

With care, all these tools will last a lifetime. Naturally the water size, gum ammoniac and gold leaf will need to be replenished from time to time.

A richly gilded illuminated initial.

Method

1. Applying gold leaf must be done on a flat, clean surface.

2. Make sure all your materials are to hand and your design or letter drawn out, ready to begin.

3. Stir the size well, then apply it evenly to the design or letter. If tiny bubbles start to appear, prick them with a pin. Leave for fifteen minutes, until it is tacky.

4. Breathe gently on the gold size, then lay the gold leaf over the top of the design. Press down all over with your burnisher, lift off the paper and gently brush off any odd bits of gold with a soft brush. Save these pieces of gold and store them in a clean jar.

5. Lastly, gently go over the gold letter or design with the agate burnisher until it shines brightly.

Reproduction

In mediaeval times, of course, all work done by illuminators was unique – a 'one-off' design. Much of my work is, too, but sometimes an occasion will demand many copies of the same design: for example, a wedding invitation, or perhaps Christmas cards. It would simply not be practical for me to paint each one individually when such large numbers are required.

At such times I may make use of modern technology such as the printing press or even the photocopier!

I have had my Christmas cards printed at my high-street print shop, which was not too expensive and gave me a large supply of my own cards. A cheaper alternative might be to have, say, a border printed in outline only, *i.e.* in black and white, and to hand-paint the coloured sections required to bring the design to life. Hand-coloured prints have, after all, a long and honourable history.

If painting involves too much time (and when you have a hundred wedding invitations to colour, this might well be the case!), simply colour in tiny parts of the design, such as rosebuds. Even just highlighting the design in gold can be extremely effective.

A photocopying machine has its uses, although the paper it copies on is really too thin to paint on if there are any large areas to colour (thin paper will cockle when it gets wet). You could try copying on to thin card – most machines will take it.

Finally, do not forget the colour photocopier, which these days is to be found in many larger public libraries as well as in copy shops. A good model can produce some excellent results.

1. The plain black design drawn in Indian ink.

2. The drawing has been duplicated and small sections of the design have been hand coloured with watercolour.

3. The fully coloured design, as you could reproduce it either by using a local printer or by using a colour photocopier.

Design

The world of nature offers you a thousand wonderful ideas for designs. Take inspiration from flowers, sea-shells, waves, insects, birds, butterflies and countless other glories, and transform their shapes and glowing colours into a unique design to decorate the things around you, from writing paper and birthday cards to jewellery boxes and paperweights.

Now that I am lucky enough to live in the countryside, surrounded by the wild flowers that grow in the fields and hedgerows, I have inspiration close to hand, but even when I lived near London, I had a flower-garden visited by various butterflies and birds which I could observe to help me in my work. Simply take time to look around you. Study the beauty of the natural world, then try to transfer something of what you see on to your paper, capturing the lovely colours and forms found in nature.

Also, look in your local library and see if you can borrow a book which shows how early scribes used design to enhance their lettering. This may give you some ideas and inspire you to create your own designs. One of the greatest books of those produced by mediaeval calligraphers and illuminators is the famous *Book of Kells*. The beauty of this ancient Irish volume has fascinated generations of historians and artists.

If you study the mediaeval illuminators' designs you will see that much thought was given to the harmonious use of colour and design, with nature being an important source of inspiration. Entwined hemp designs are a recurrent motif and are reflected in some of these Celtic borders and letters.

Design changes with the times, but William Morris and Owen Jones, both masters of their craft, still influence the designs on our upholstery, furnishings and dress fabrics to this day. Owen Jones found inspiration in the designs of Oriental, Persian, Greek, Arab and Indian artists. Other influences from the past include ancient Greece

Stylised lilies entwined with initials.

A Chinese-style design with salamanders.

and Egypt, which are reflected in the angular designs of the 1920s and 1930s.

Using ideas of your own, and looking around at nature, try to create designs that are personal to you. You will get great satisfaction from creating something original that you have painted in lovely toning colours.

Remember that every design, whether on a useful item or simply a beautiful decorative border surrounding a well-written text or verse, is a work of art in itself. You can treasure it always, or you can give someone great pleasure by passing it on as a welcome gift.

How to develop a design

Designing stylised patterns from the original source can be a lot of fun, and also you can get some really stunning results. Over the next few pages you will see how the designs develop from the 'original' object.

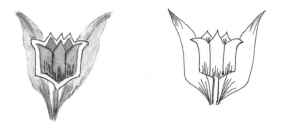

Tulips

Tulips are very easy to use for creating wonderful designs because of the distinctive shape of the flower. Here I have used the tulip in a running border as well as for a design which could be suitable as a kitchen tile or a table mat.

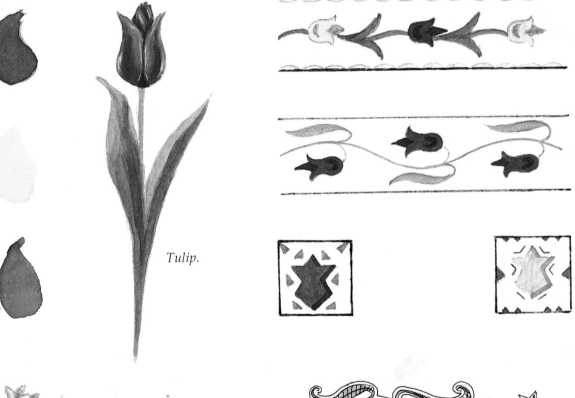

Tulip.

The tulip: inspiration for a number of different designed borders and motifs.

Rose.

*Running border
of rosebuds.*

*Rosebud motif for a
tile, or as a corner
where two borders
meet.*

*A designed border of
stylised full-face
roses.*

*Stylised rose: taking
the stylisation to its
utmost limit.*

Roses

Roses are deservedly popular and make charm-
ing borders, whether represented as a border of
realistic pink or red rosebuds with their fresh
green leaves, or stylised into almost geometric
motifs. The Tudor rose is another development
of the theme.

Poppies

The lovely colour contrast of the red poppy and its green foliage attracted me to design two very different but equally effective borders.

The flowers are still quite naturalistic in this pretty poppy border.

Poppy.

Here I have stylised the poppies further and created a kind of stained-glass-effect border with very clear colours, using gouache.

Violets

I have started with a single flower, then stylised the violets into a range of useful designs.

Apple blossom

Here I have developed a spray of delicate pink-and-white apple blossom into a decorative border.

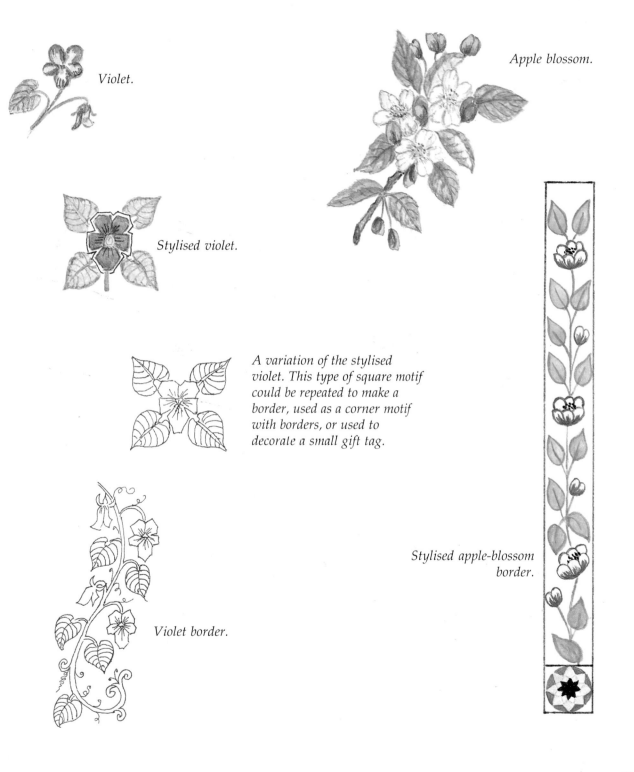

Violet.

Apple blossom.

Stylised violet.

A variation of the stylised violet. This type of square motif could be repeated to make a border, used as a corner motif with borders, or used to decorate a small gift tag.

Violet border.

Stylised apple-blossom border.

Apples

Some fruit can also be an excellent source of a design. For example, cut an apple in half and look at the pattern formed by the pips inside. It suggests a wheel to me: perhaps you can see a different picture or design in half an apple, or half an orange?

A border of apples and apple blossom, together with a corner motif echoing the pattern of the pips.

Apple.

If you look at half an apple, you can see the regular pattern formed by the dark pips in the white circle of the cut apple.

Two stylised designs suggested by half an apple.

Butterflies and bugs

Illuminators in the past used animals, insects and sea creatures as the basis for fantastic or even rather gross designs. I have created some butterfly and insect-based designs to give you further ideas. Really, the possibilities are endless!

Swallow-tail butterfly.

A naturalistic butterfly border.

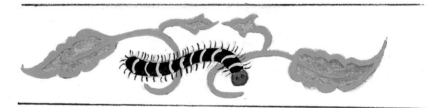

An idea for a caterpillar border!

Stylised butterfly.

Three butterfly borders.

Sea creatures

I had great fun with these sea creatures. One has only to look at the nature programmes on television to see how Nature herself has created the most amazing colourful and outlandish designs in her denizens of the deep.

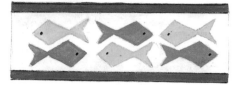

A shoal of stylised fish swims happily along this border. A motif as simple as this could easily be made into a stencil to decorate a bathroom wall.

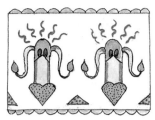

An idea for a border of flying squid.

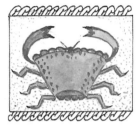

A stylised crab motif.

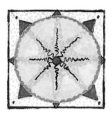

Jellyfish motif.

A lyrefish border.

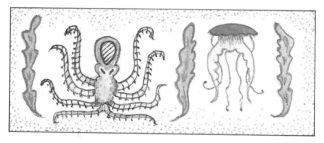

A border of jellyfish, seaweed and octopi.

Swordfish motifs.

A border of plaice and shells.
Note the bubble motifs and the wave edging – all part of the theme!

A stylised starfish motif.

Repeating motifs

These 'snowflake' motifs are very useful. You can decorate your work with them, or you can repeat them round a piece of written text to form a very attractive border. Use a technical pen to get the thin, delicate lines they require, and add watercolour where you need some colour.

A border composed of repeated snowflake motifs.

Six snowflake designs.

Shadowing

Adding shadows to a painted flower or piece of foliage can heighten interest and will also give an almost three-dimensional effect.

First paint your chosen subject – take a real pansy, rose, lily or whatever to copy from – and then add a subtle shadow to make the painted flower really stand out. To do this, shine a bright light on your subject and then observe the shadows the light throws behind the flower. Simply add these to your painting.

If you are left-handed, place the light to your right and above your subject. As I am right-handed, I shine the light from above and the left.

Here I have painted a simple example of a daffodil using this method. On page 60 you can see a much more complicated example: a full-page painting of pansies and fuchsias.

You could also experiment with subtle variants of the colour of the shadow to see which looks best: a plain cool grey, a touch of blue to complement a yellow flower, or a bluish purple to go with a red flower.

A daffodil painted using the shadowing technique.

21

Stippling

Stippling is an ancient way of adding depth or colour to paintings and drawings. The illuminators of the *Book of Kells* used it quite extensively in their manuscripts, as did scribes during the Middle Ages; and the Impressionists, hundreds of years later, adapted the technique.

The modern painters Georges Seurat and Paul Signac used this technique extensively, calling it pointillism. *The Bathers,* which can be seen in the National Gallery in London, is a very good example of Seurat's work.

The method was also often used in engravings to produce half-tones and delicate lines, and is still used in commercial illustration.

Pointillism can be carried out in a very delicate way, using fine paintbrushes, or in a very broad manner, using your fingers to dab on oil, acrylic or even pastel to give shading and depth to a painting. I use a form of pointillism in all my portrait paintings in miniature: I place dots of paint on the vellum, then soften the edges of the dots to blend into a smooth surface.

In this book I have used stippling quite a lot, especially on my ciphers and monograms.

Pointillism is seen at its best when you use pure bright colours. Blended together, these numerous dots will produce a very much brighter effect than mixing, say, yellow and blue to produce green. Laying dots of pure yellow in juxtaposition with pure blue will result in a bright and very startling green.

When viewing a pointillist painting you must hold the painting at a certain distance from your eye to produce the right effect; then the eye, when looking at the two colours side by side, will get the illusion of green.

I have used stippling in some of my borders and ciphers to give a 'shading' effect to the finished work. I thought the backgrounds to some of the ciphers mounted on shields looked rather bare, so I decided to use stippling to give depth and interest to the overall effect of the final design.

If you have painted a colour that rather jumps

I used a very highly finished version of stippling to create this delicate watercolour picture, which is painted on vellum. The dots are so fine that you can hardly see them unless you look closely.

out at you, such as a bright red or a sharp alizarin green, and you feel you would like to soften it, you can do so by using a light-grey fibre-tipped pen. You will find that this sends the colour back into the painting.

A stylo-tip is particularly suitable for this technique as its tubular nib produces neat dots of equal size, and nibs are available in different sizes. You can even buy an electrically powered stippling pen!

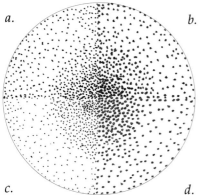

a.

b.

In this circle, which I divided into four sections, I used a very fine black technical pen in (a) and a black fibre-tipped pen in (b). I did the same in red in (c) and (d).

This shows how a quick freehand design can be easily created by the use of dots of various colours over a thin wash of watercolour.

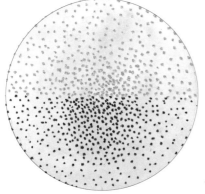

c.

d.

First I painted a thin wash of alizarin green, then I heightened one half with a yellow fibre-tipped pen and the other half with a pure-blue fibre-tipped pen.

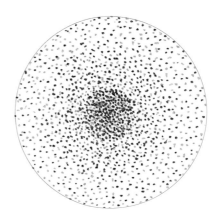

Here you can see how the use of red, yellow and blue dots, graduated at random, can give the illusion, when viewed at a distance, of brown.

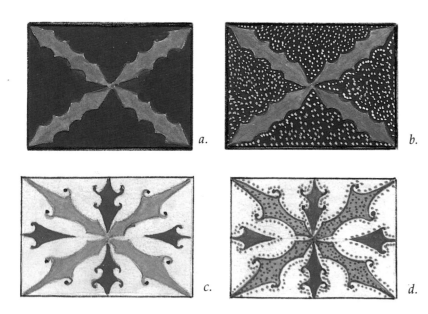

a.

b.

c.

d.

An example of the way stippling can soften the harshness of a colour: I felt that the stylised holly design in (a) was rather drowned by the brightness of the red, so to soften it I dotted white paint all over the background with a fine brush (b). This gave the impression of snowflakes and also brought the green holly forward.

The stylised holly design in (c) looked perfectly well balanced colour-wise, but I decided that by using stippling on the pale holly leaves I could add interest and strengthen the design (d).

One design – three different media

I painted the same design three times, each time using a different medium.

(a) After drawing the design I outlined everything with a mapping pen, using vermilion paint. I then painted parts of the design with water gold size (see page 11 for instructions on gilding). When this was ready, I applied the gold leaf, tidied up the edges with my soft brush, and, finally, burnished the gold.

(b) The second design is painted using water-colour pencil. First I outlined the parts to be filled in with an appropriately coloured pencil; then, with a nearly dry brush, I painted the various colours, starting from the outside in each case and working inwards. When this was dry, I shaded parts of the design with a darker colour. Except when extra colour is applied for darkening purposes, the paper should always show through the paint.

(c) I used gouache for this design and you will notice that the paint is more solid, but still not too heavy. Gouache can be manipulated if it is handled carefully.

If you find these designs are too delicate to practise with, then you could draw some similar designs on a much larger scale and practise using one of these media on those.

a.

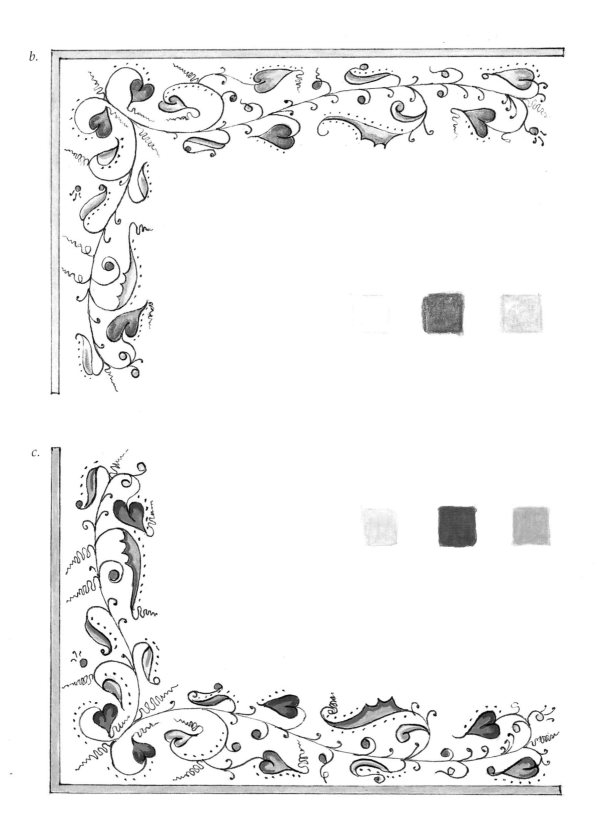

b.

c.

Coloured papers

Although watercolour is my favourite medium (I use it in all my fine work: for miniature portraits and for delicate work such as borders for my calligraphy), when I use coloured papers I need more body colour and I may choose gouache.

As I described in the section on *Choosing paints*, gouache is easier to work with than watercolour, especially as it does not streak. (If you have to stop work temporarily, you can easily resume your painting without leaving a tidemark as you would with watercolour.) The colours are usually very brilliant and strong. Do not mix them, as they may turn out muddy; it is better to buy a tube of the colour you require.

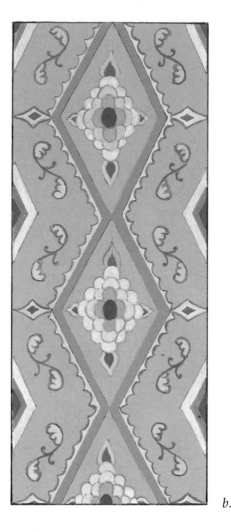

b.

a.

Eventually, however, I decided to use watercolour: Chinese white, with the addition of some colour to tint it. I used only two colours in each study, the colour of the paper dictating my choice of colours, and by adding varying amounts of Chinese white to those two colours I obtained the various tints you see here. I then highlighted each design with gold leaf.

I chose a paeony as my main motif, and, using its opened-flat petals, I set out the design with a leaf shape at the top and sides of the flower motif, and also filling the gap between the central band and the outer edge. The colours are of course not the true colours of the paeony or its leaves, but are chosen to suit the paper.

First of all I drew the paeony design on some copy paper, then transferred it on to each piece of coloured paper by tracing.

c.

d.

(a) On the pink paper, I used Chinese white, mixed with first some alizarin-green watercolour to make pale green, and, second, alizarin crimson to make pink. I painted the pink areas first, gradually adding a little more colour for the darker shades of the paeony and the surrounding sections of the design. Then I did the same with the green parts of the design.

When all the paint was thoroughly dry, I gently erased all the pencil lines and applied the gold leaf, then burnished it and tidied up the edges of the gold borders.

Lastly, I drew a line in ink round the outer edge of the design with a technical pen. (I used this same procedure for all four designs).

(b) Here I used Chinese white with alizarin green and with vermilion, this time on blue paper. You will see how the colour of the background dictates the colour of your paints; subtle combinations always look best.

(c) On the grey paper, I used Chinese white mixed with alizarin crimson and with violet, and also Chinese white used alone.

(d) I used tints of orange and alizarin green to tone down the yellow of the paper, as I found this yellow rather too vivid.

Study the effect of the colour schemes against the coloured paper, then experiment with your own colours and paper, but try not to use too many colours at first. Also, check that one colour does not stand out more than the others, putting the rest of the design in the shade.

Keep a certain balance and harmony with your colours and choice of paper. You will soon find that with a little practice, colour mixing will become quite simple.

USING ILLUMINATED DESIGNS

Greetings cards

Nice cards can be expensive to buy, especially at Christmas when you need so many of them. Try making your own cards, with the appropriate message done in hand-written calligraphy.

When designing your own hand-painted greetings cards or labels, to begin with you should try to keep them all very simple: do not be tempted to use too many colours at once, or you could end up with a rather garish look.

The decorative classic design above would be suitable for any occasion, for a man or for a woman. You could glue it to a piece of toning or contrasting card in such a way that the card forms a border all round the design panel.

Inside the card, depending on its colour, you could either write your greeting on the card itself, or, if you think the ink would not show up sufficiently, on a white paper insert.

Greetings card in watercolour on vellum. The lighthouse is based on one in Happisburgh, Norfolk.

You can buy 'blank' cards in the shops to use for any occasion you like: this sort of pretty but non-thematic design is suitable for use as a blank card.

I painted the card above on vellum using watercolour, and mounted it on a card that toned in with the colours of the painting. The poppy border is a development of that on page 16.

The oval-shaped motif is an excellent one to use: you can frame it prettily with curving flowers, or paint an elegant classic border around it. For framing, you can buy oval-shaped mounts which you can choose in a colour that will tone with your painting.

On the right I have painted an alternative oval design in the same style, showing a Norfolk windmill surrounded by a symmetrical border of spring tulips (the tulips are from my garden).

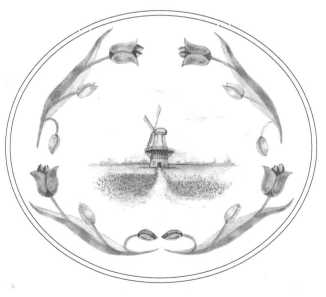

Idea for another oval greetings-card motif in watercolour.

29

Valentine card painted in gouache. I have also painted a complementary motif to decorate the flap of the envelope, using watercolour and felt-tip pen.

Valentine card

If ever there was an occasion that called for a lovingly hand-painted card, surely it is St Valentine's Day!

The card is painted in gouache, with the lacy edging outlined with a fine technical pen. In the centre, you could letter 'Be my Valentine', 'Be Mine', 'To my Valentine', or a similar Victorian sentiment, to match the style of the card.

If you were really clever, you could devise some way of making the whole card heart-shaped, although it probably would not have much of a hinge, but I suspect a heart-shaped envelope would probably defeat you!

At the top of the page I have also painted a motif on a romantic pale-pink envelope to go with the card.

Birthday card

On this page I have created a greetings card, painted in gouache, for a birthday (although the scroll could actually be lettered with anything from 'Happy Birthday' to 'Best Wishes', or even 'Congratulations', as the design is not composed of cakes and balloons!).

I have used soft, well-balanced colours which go well together: a particularly good choice for a card with a gentle, pretty theme. The summer flowers, broderie anglaise and lace all combine to underline the air of femininity.

This type of design would also make a lovely card for Mother's Day.

Birthday card.

Christmas card

Simplicity is always effective. For instance, this Christmas card is really quite plain, consisting of a single decorated word and a toning border, but the colour selection ties it all together and makes it work.

I had this card printed by our local printer and I now have my own Christmas cards at a fraction of the price I would have had to pay for them in the shops.

Christmas card.

Gift cards

I always enjoy painting gift cards – they offer wonderful opportunities for miniature work and are quickly done due to their small size. They really do finish off a beautifully wrapped present well, and of course you can match the colour of the wrapping paper and ribbon if you like. (In that case it is probably best to use paper that is plain rather than patterned).

A delicate flowery design suitable for many occasions, or indeed for presenting with a bouquet.

This gift card was drawn in Indian ink and then the colour was added with watercolour. You could add 'Greetings' or 'Happy Birthday' in calligraphy, or just leave it plain for your handwritten message.

I painted this Christmas gift card in watercolour, with a design of holly and Christmas roses.

Oval wine label in watercolour.

Rectangular wine label.

Labels

There is no reason why you could not draw your labels on self-adhesive paper and stick them on pots of home-made jam or pickles. Or what about painting your own labels for your home-made wine, as I have done here? I have used stylised bunches of grapes, but if you make country wine, there are many design ideas to be found in dandelions, cowslips, blackberries and all the other wild flowers and fruits that you can use.

Stationery

Personal writing paper

Making yourself some lovely writing paper is really easy. Choose your favourite colours – you can buy a lovely range of subtle colours in stationers' shops, and you can get sheets individually, with envelopes to match – and then simply add a monogram, motif, or border: as little or as much work as you like. Combine some of the square snowflake motifs shown on page 21 to make a corner motif, or go right round the page with them, or place your initial in a decorative box and illuminate it, as I have done on page 36. Use gold to bring your design to life if you like, or paint ribbons and flowers....

Why not paint a miniature picture of your friends' house to decorate their personal stationery and have it printed, as I have done below? This sort of personalised present is much appreciated. (A variation on this theme is the picture of the church in which a couple are to be married, to be printed on a wedding invitation, which has become fashionable of late.)

Instead of paper, you could make some correspondence cards for a change. These are available in white, cream, pastel shades, or even with gold edges.

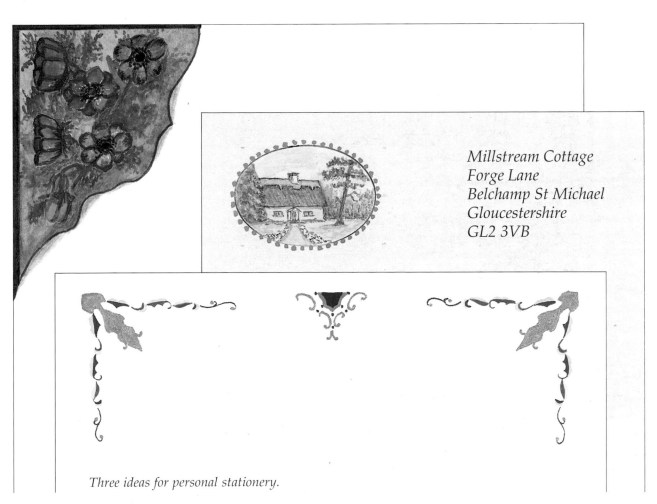

Millstream Cottage
Forge Lane
Belchamp St Michael
Gloucestershire
GL2 3VB

Three ideas for personal stationery.

Here I have painted an
elegant illuminated initial in
watercolour for a friend's
personalised writing paper.

A special touch
would be an
envelope with a
matching motif on
the point of the
back flap.

Business stationery

There are many opportunities for a designer to create specialised business stationery for various trades and professions: the gardener, the calligrapher, the caterer, the dressmaker.... Here I have designed some for a florist and have had it typeset.

Business stationery specially designed for a florist: letter-head, business card, and blank gift card to be presented with a bouquet.

56 Lavender Walk, Great Bentley, Colchester, Essex, CO7 8PH
Telephone: (0206) 250 218

Flowers by Clare

Jenny Thorpe
56 Lavender Walk
Great Bentley
Colchester
Essex
CO7 8PH

Tel. (0206) 250 218

The wedding

A wedding gives endless opportunities for beautiful designs, starting with the invitation and going on to the decorative title page for the wedding album. Calligraphers will probably already have found that one of the most common requests they receive is to letter the front of someone's album!

I have given an idea for a wedding invitation, a place card, and a title page. If you are designing place cards for a large wedding, you might like to confine the special ones to the 'top table' and stick to plain calligraphy for the rest, unless your energy is unlimited! The wedding invitations, of course, have been printed, as so many of them are required.

Place card.

Mr and Mrs C.W. May
request the pleasure of your company on the
occasion of the marriage of their daughter
Laura Felicity
to
Hilary John St George de Vere

at 2.00pm on 23rd June, 1994,
at All Saints' Church, Thornham Parva,
and afterwards at
the County Hotel, Wheaton.

R.S.V.P.

Wedding invitation.

Title page for an album of wedding photographs.

38

The Marriage of

Laura Felicity May
and
Hilary John St George
de Vere on
23rd June 1994
at All Saints' Church
Thornham Parva

The celebration dinner party

Anniversary, golden wedding, engagement, or simply a romantic dinner *à deux* – why not make the occasion special by creating some lovely items?

First of all, a pretty invitation is always impressive – such things often end up adorning the invitee's mantelpiece for months after the event has come and gone. For this example I have designed a border of stylised pansies in watercolour, with a stippled background.

At the dinner-table, it is a nice touch to designate seating by hand-made place cards. Write your guests' names in flowing calligraphy, or use a gold marker. This one is painted to match the invitation.

You could even make coasters for the table, if you have time. (You could make the place cards match your coasters, if you liked.) A good stationer could probably make you up a set of these, but you would have to order a large number of them for it to be economical.

Place card.

An invitation, handwritten in elegant italic script.

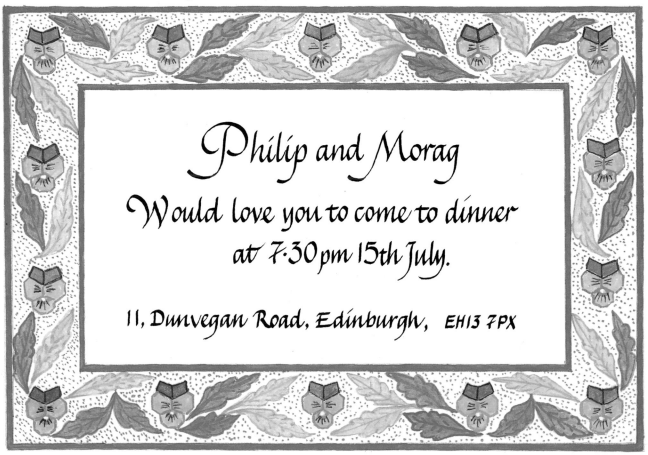

40

Menu

It is rather fun to design a menu for a special occasion, as one might find for a function at a top hotel. In fact, your skills might even be in demand at a local restaurant! This menu has been typeset, but hand-written menus in attractive calligraphy are appropriate in less formal establishments.

Menu.

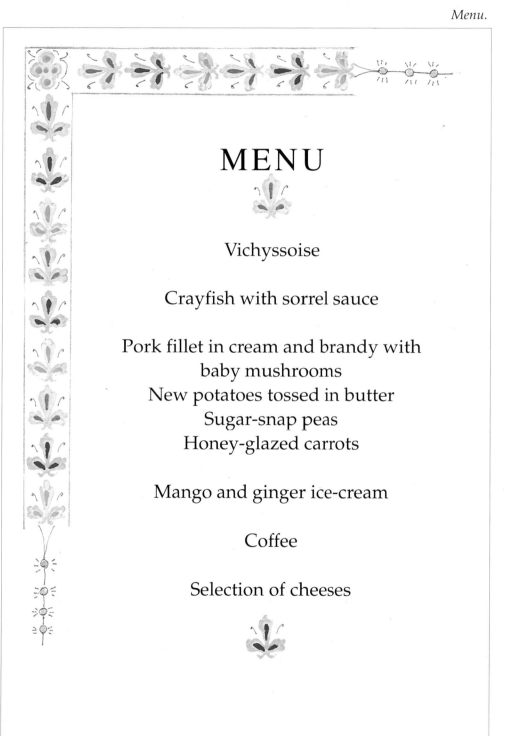

MENU

Vichyssoise

Crayfish with sorrel sauce

Pork fillet in cream and brandy with
baby mushrooms
New potatoes tossed in butter
Sugar-snap peas
Honey-glazed carrots

Mango and ginger ice-cream

Coffee

Selection of cheeses

Birthday book

A rather larger project, if you have the time, would be to create your own birthday book in a small bound book of blank paper, such as are sold as a superior sort of notebook. You could have a different design for each month, or even each week if you wanted.

This design, for a single page of the birthday book, is done in gouache and outlined in fibre-tipped pen. For a finished-looking result, you could use rub-down lettering for the wording you require.

You could also create a rather splendid desk diary in this manner.

Address book

Similarly, a small notebook could be decorated with twenty-six simple illuminated capital letters to create an address book or book for writing down important telephone numbers.

Address book.

Birthday book.

Decorative items

Paperweights and box-lids

A paperweight or little box is a lovely way to show off your best work. You can buy blank glass paperweights in craft shops – you simply put your design underneath the glass. On a box-lid, you could either place a piece of glass (cut to size) on top of the design to protect it, or varnish it carefully.

The four illuminated initials on this page are painted in watercolour and gouache, with the addition of gold, while the filigree leaf backgrounds in designs 1, 3, and 4 are outlined in ink. All these designs are suitable for box-lids, but the round and oval designs will be easier to make into paperweights than the square ones. The thing to do is to buy the paperweight blank before you plan your design, and simply make it fit in the first place.

1.

2.

3.

4.

Four designs for paperweights and box-lids.

Box lid painted in gouache and gold leaf, with a stippled background.

This intricate design for a box-lid is painted in gouache. If you used acrylics, you could paint directly on to the box itself, but remember to varnish your work to protect it.

This delicate design with its decorative capital letter took quite a lot of work, but it makes a lovely lid for a jewellery box and would be a personalised gift to treasure.

Monograms and ciphers

Monograms and ciphers are personalised and attractive – what better excuse to try a few out?

As a painter of miniature portraits I scoured the book shops and libraries for ideas on how to design a monogram – to no avail. I decided I would have to create my own designs. Not so easy as you might think, bearing in mind that I wanted to produce something simple and neat. However, I did succeed in creating a personal monogram, which you can see below.

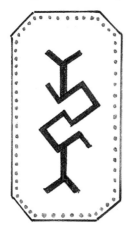

This is my personal monogram, which I use (without the border) to sign all my work. (My art books are published under the name of 'Patricia Carter', but my full name is J.P. Carter.)

It is nice to have one for yourself, but they are also sometimes required by large businesses, colleges and societies to use as letterheads, on envelopes and on posters. In fact, designing monograms for commercial advertising is an occupation of its own. They make good logos too.

On your way round the shops, look at various products and you may spot monograms on a lot of items, such as jars of jams and other bottled foodstuffs. You will also see them on labels attached to clothing. A lot of societies, too, have a monogram of some sort.

Ciphers are similar to monograms, but they are usually written in very elaborately entwined letters. Unless you are the owner of the cipher, it is almost impossible to decipher some of them! They are sometimes stamped on jewellery boxes, snuff boxes and other personal items belonging to a family, and are a very personal thing.

How to design a monogram

Take a piece of coloured wool and form it into the shape of a letter. Take another length of wool of a different colour, and interweave a second letter with the first. This may be all you require, but if a third letter is required, then weave in yet another letter, in a different colour.

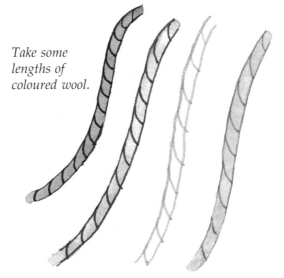

Take some lengths of coloured wool.

These woollen letter-shapes can now be moved round until you have all the letters arranged in a design that you like. You could also try cutting out some thin letter shapes in paper and weaving these in and out of one another.

Shape the pieces of wool into an interwoven monogram.

Make a pencil sketch of your monogram.

Here you can see the finished monogram.

Once you have got all the letters arranged in the design you find most satisfactory, make a pencil sketch of them on paper. Then carefully draw the letters for your final version, and apply your choice of paint, ink, or felt-tip to colour your design.

These three monograms are drawn and filled in with coloured fibre-tipped pens.

All the ciphers on this page have been drawn and filled in with fibre-tips, and the scroll around the 'GP' cipher is shaded with watercolour.

Bookmarks

Any long, thin design will be suitable for a bookmark. You can vary the shape of the card when you are cutting it out, and tailor the design to suit the shape: a curvilinear design, for example, will go well with a shape with a curved lower end and perhaps rounded corners.

You could add a length of toning narrow ribbon to the bottom of the bookmark, so as to mark your place in the book more visibly (thread it through a small punched hole in the card and knot it in place).

In (a), a rich swag of ripe fruit decorates this unusual-shaped bookmark with its lacy scalloped top edge and gently curving lower edge. The fruit is painted in watercolour, as are the pale leaf motifs that fill the border.

The scroll-shaped pictorial bookmark for an artist, (b), is painted in watercolour.

You will also find that a classic design makes an elegant and stylish bookmark (c). There are endless variations on this theme.

a.

b.

c.

Bookplates

Bookplates were very popular from Victorian times right up until the 1930s, when austerity swept the design world. Recently, however, they have been coming back in a big way.

Bookplates are both attractive and useful. They remind people who borrow your books who to give them back to, and decorate the inside cover of your books rather stylishly. Some people also write the date they bought the book on the bookplate, as a reminder for years to come.

You can also use bookplates for occasions such as prize-givings: letter the prizewinner's name and the prize the book denotes on the bookplate in attractive calligraphy before the presentation.

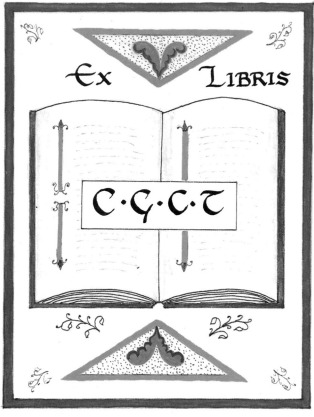

A formal bookplate executed in watercolour. I used an ordinary ballpoint pen for the stippled backgrounds and gouache for the outer border.

You may have noticed boxes or blocks of bookplates with gummed backs that just have to be moistened and stuck into a book. I have seen them in good stationers' and in gift shops in stately homes open to the public. They can be expensive when purchased from shops, but if you design your own and have a number of copies run off by a printer, they will last you for many a year.

The lettering could consist of 'This book belongs to', or 'From the library of', or the Latin *Ex Libris*, which means exactly the same. Then just add the name of the owner of the book – Christian name, or surname as well, or initials and surname.

You can create a classic decorative design, or

This simple but effective design was created with a pair of compasses and edged with gold. The colours were carefully graduated.

you can personalise your bookplates with a design that reflects your own interests. If you prepare one for a friend, you could incorporate in the design something relevant to your friend's hobby – or indeed the subject of the book you are giving your friend with the bookplate already in place, such as fishing tackle, a spanner (for a mechanic), or some musical notation (for a musician). With a little imagination, you can think up many other ideas and themes.

Apart from the one-off special bookplate, you could have a supply of personalised bookplates printed for a friend – what a marvellous present!

Classic designs

The classic Florentine design makes an elegant bookplate. Here I have painted the delicate flowers and leaves in watercolour: the design represents a stylised rosebud and is done freehand, while gold is used for the border and to highlight the design.

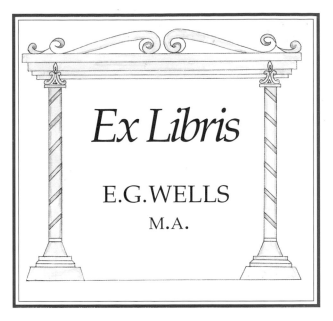

This stern architectural design would suit a gentleman's library. I drew it using drawing inks, a fine nib and a ruler, and had it printed.

Leaves and scrolls make a suitable bookplate for anyone. Add a plain border, or a leafy one, or an oval one if you want to be a bit different. Here I have used gouache and a pen.

If you have a family crest, it would make a splendid bookplate, and one that could be used by all your family. It would be worth while having some printed. Heraldic emblems in general are very decorative, but if you are making up an imaginary crest, make sure you have not inadvertently purloined somebody else's!

For the sailing enthusiast, I have incorporated a ship, a ship's wheel, and some rope into the design, which is painted in gouache on coloured paper.

Various writing and drawing implements adorn this bookplate for a schoolboy or student, which I have painted in gouache on green writing paper.

Personalised designs

Whatever interests you or your friends may have, you are likely to be able to design a special bookplate on the same theme: music, art, archery, gardening, butterfly-collecting, bee-keeping, or ballet. Here I have painted some examples for a sailor and a schoolboy.

You can also have fun designing a bookplate around someone's name, as I have done with Mr Heron (bottom left), if you can make some kind of visual association (heraldic coats of arms sometimes used this idea). Think what you could do with the following surnames: Fox, Archer, Nightingale, Bridgewater, Falconer, Brooke, Hare, Rose, Sparrow...

This is another bookplate for the hobby sailor, showing a yacht on the Norfolk Broads, near where I live, and a stylised heron. I have painted it in watercolour.

53

Decorative title pages

Many books have a decorative title page. It tells you the
title of the book, the author's name and the publisher.
According to the subject of the book, this may be ornate
or plain; historical or modern. A good decorative title
page may entice you into opening the pages of
a book and reading on.

For instance, a remembrance book which lists the names
of deceased servicemen would probably have a decorative
border and a national flag, and perhaps the badge of the
particular branch of the services, such as the
Army, Navy or RAF.

Books on gardening, needlework, art, or other crafts
might have a frontispiece linked to that theme, while
serious books, such as educational ones, might be simpler
and more sober. Whatever your subject-matter, first
consider whether you are aiming for an ultra-modern
frontispiece or one that is more traditional.

Why not decorate the front of a christening photograph
album as a present, or the title page of a friend's wedding
album? I have found that there is quite
a demand for such work.

How to design a decorative title page

Choose a design for the page and make a rough sketch of it. Now measure the page, leaving a border all round, with a slightly larger border at the bottom of the page (having a slightly wider border at the bottom of the page than the top gives a balance to the page). Divide the page in half lengthwise to give a guideline for the title and any other wording, then letter the title, author's name, etc.

Next, measure a box at each corner for your border, then draw a border design lightly in pencil. Paint each colour separately in each corner, working from the outside and using a spare piece of paper to rest your hand on to avoid smudging the inked wording (if you have not used Indian ink). Any gold should be added after you have finished painting, unless you have a gold capital letter in the title.

Finally, when all the paint is thoroughly dry, erase the pencil lines carefully.

Colophons

A colophon is the inscription at the end of a book, giving the sort of details now more usually found on the title page. In a personalised book this might be the church, or crematorium, or a private benefactor. Until the 1920s some of these colophons were extremely decorative, but when the austerity of Art Deco took over, books became plainer and more utilitarian in appearance. A more romantic trend is now becoming apparent in design and in the art world generally, and colophons are staging a bit of a comeback.

I am often asked to letter, decorate, and illuminate remembrance books, and these always require a colophon. Sometimes I use an historical border, but I also like to design modern ones. It all depends on the type of book I am working on at the time. If a military body has commissioned me to letter a book, then this theme may be reflected in the design of the colophon.

Colophons are not difficult to design. The best thing to do is to jot down the wording and see if it fits into a triangle, square, oval or oblong shape. The rest will fall into place and ideas will soon materialise.

I think it is appropriate for me to finish this section by designing a colophon for this book!

This Remembrance Book was given to the Lowestoft Branch of the Burma Star Association by A·H· Carter and written and illuminated by J·P· Carter 1991

Colophon for a remembrance book.

Colophon.

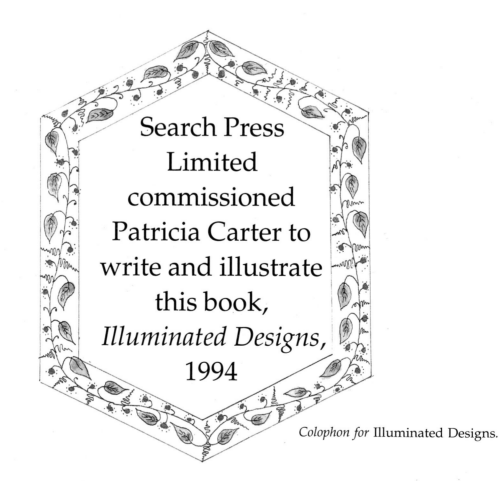

Search Press Limited commissioned Patricia Carter to write and illustrate this book, *Illuminated Designs,* 1994

Colophon for Illuminated Designs.

Illuminated texts

Texts, poems and favourite sayings are grist to every calligrapher's mill, and there are innumerable possibilities for decorative borders, whether classic or themed to go with the text. For example, a religious text could have a stained-glass border; or a poem about spring might look good with a frame of primroses and violets. Simply choose your favourite text, saying, quotation or short poem and think about what sort of design might suit it.

On this page and pages 60 and 62 I have designed some classic borders for use with any text; on page 59 I have illuminated a quotation about snow with wintry scenes; and on page 63 I have painted a thoroughly Chinese border with dragons, to go with a Chinese saying. The shell border on page 61 was designed to complement a poem about a shell.

All the decorative skills you have learnt in this book can be shown off in a splendid border!

Snow
 doesn't fall
To lose us all
But so that every creature
 However frail
 Declares its trail.

Siberian Saying

Words
without
thoughts
never to
heaven
go

Hamlet

MY HEART IS LIKE
    A RAINBOW SHELL
THAT PADDLES IN A
    HALCYON SEA;

MY HEART IS GLADDER
THAN ALL THESE
BECAUSE MY LOVE
    IS COME TO ME

CHRISTINA ROSSETTI

thou shalt
LOVE
thy
NEIGHBOUR
as thyself

Matthew XIX·19

If a man acts
with a pure
thought,
happiness follows
him like a
shadow that
never
leaves him.

BUDDHA

Index